Raspb

*New Users Programming
Raspberry Pi 3 Guide with
Raspberry Pi 3 Projects*

Josh Thompsons

book are for clarifying purposes only and are the owned by the owners themselves, not affiliated with this document.

CONTENTS

Introduction

I want to thank you and congratulate you for purchasing the book, *"Raspberry Pi 3: New Users Programming Raspberry Pi 3 Guide with Raspberry Pi 3 Projects."*

This book contains proven steps and strategies on how to get started with your Raspberry Pi 3, how to program it and some of the more useful projects that you can build with it.

The Raspberry Pi 3 is, without a doubt, the most popular microcomputer in the world and was originally released for teaching. Now, it is mostly used by those who love to program and who love to build things but it is still the ideal platform for those who want to learn how to program.

Thanks again for purchasing this book, I hope you enjoy it!

Chapter 1: Raspberry Pi 3 Basics

The Raspberry Pi is one of the most popular computer systems of all time, despite the fact that it is no bigger than a credit card. It was designed originally for education, for teaching young people how to get started in programming and its inspiration came from the BBC Micro, produced in 1981. The goal was to give users a cost-effective device that would help in the improvement of programming skills and understanding hardware but, thanks to the tiny size and the incredibly small price tag, Raspberry Pi was soon taken on by electronics enthusiasts for use in all manner of different projects, some of which we will talk about later.

Raspberry Pi is not as fast as a modern desktop or laptop but it is still an entire Linux system and it can give you all the abilities you expect in a computer at a lower level of power consumption. The boards are made in Wales in the UK, with the first model, the Raspberry Pi 1 Model A being released in 2012. Model B came out later on in 2012 although this is the one that most people say is the original. Model B had all the features on it that the creators wanted to be included while Model A was seen as a cheaper model, a preview that could match Model B if extra peripherals were added to it. Both models were the same size and had the same processor.

Model B+ was the more advanced version of Model A+, containing better memory, a faster rate of processing and lower costs. These were the models that were adopted by schools, the models that taught students how to study computer science and be more innovative. Many forums on the internet today show just how creative some of these students have been with the projects they have devised.

In February 2015, Raspberry Pi 2 was released and Model B was an amalgamation of all the best features from the first models, along with much-needed improvements. Most of the projects and the software needed can be done on all models of the Pi, making it incredibly convenient and, if you have an older model and are not able to upgrade, it means you don't have to. However, upgrading to the latest model is advisable if you want to get the best out of it.

The Raspberry Pi 3 Model B is the latest and has the fastest processor and the best memory of all the models. Its user interface, graphic specifications, and connectivity are far superior to the earlier models and there are other features that make it the one to buy:

Technical Specifications:

- Bluetooth 4.1

- Wi-Fi 802.11n

- 1GB SDRAM

- 1.2 GHz quad-core processor – 64-bit Broadcom ARM 48 processors

- Headphone and HDMI audio output

- Composite and HDMI video output

- 400 MHz VideoCore IV GPU

- Ethernet 10/100

- Ethernet port

- Display interface

- 2 USB ports

- Micro SD slot

- Camera interface

- 3.5 mm composite slot

Hardware

When you purchase your Raspberry Pi 3, you are buying a board and, to make it work in the ways that you want it to, you will more than likely require other peripherals. However, as the board is a computer, let's look at what it has on board to start with:

- **System on Chip** – The SoC is the chip used to for processing. It is manufactured by Broadcom and is model BCM2837 SOC, the only Pi model with this chip in it

- **CPU** – Central Processing Unit – this is a quad-core ARM A53 processor cortex. Most laptops and desktops have an A15 ARM cortex so you can see just how powerful this is. The earlier models contained the ARM 1176JZF-S chop which would work on a frequency of 700 MHz for processing the latest model, the Pi 3, has a frequency of 1.2 GHz, running on dual processing cores at 32 kb Level 1 And 512 kb Level 2 cache memory. Linked to this is the 1 GB LPDDR2 memory which you will find on the back of the board.

- **GPU** – Graphics Processing Unit – this has stayed pretty much the same across all models and is a Broadcom VideoCore IV that runs at 400 MHz with OpenGL ES – an interface specifically manufactured for embedded systems. It has compatibility with MPEG 2 and VC 1 and can also render images in 1080p. High-quality video is via the H.264/MPEG-4 AVC encoder and decoder. The graphics are equal to those found on the Xbox 360.

- **Memory** – The Raspberry Pi 3 has a MicroSD card slot and you will find that on the rear of the board. This is used as detectable memory and is what you will load your operating system and software onto, as well as external applications, documents, and files needed by the CPU and GPU while instructions are being executed.

- **RAM** – The Random Access Memory is now 1 GB, shared with the GPU and is about twice the RAM that previous models had. It uses 512 M

- B or lower with the GPU, thus enabling fast rendering of 1080p video and 3D video. The rest of the RAM is used by the CPU.

- **Ethernet and USB Ports** – The Ethernet port is used to connect the Ethernet cable, an 8 position, 8 connector (8P8C) module with a pair of terminally twisted cables, allowing access to the internet. There are 2 USB ports that you can also use for internet connection but these are usually for adding on peripherals like a mouse or a keyboard

- **Mini USB Jack -** used for a power pack

- **40 GPIO pins** – The General Purpose Input Output Pins are used for peripherals that can be customized depending on the project you are doing

- **Audio Ports** – an integrated Interchip Sound system that can connect digital devices or components

- **Camera Serial Interface** – used for connecting a camera

- **DSI** – Display Serial Interface – used for connecting an external display component, such as a television, monitor, laptop screen or another display device.

- **Wi-Fi** – 802.11n support allows the Pi 3 to be connected wirelessly to the internet, a first for any of the Pi models

- **Bluetooth** – Support for Bluetooth 41, allowing for wireless connection between devices that are in range and paired via Bluetooth – also the first Pi model to have this

- **Clock** – Pi 3 is dependent on the network time server for real-world time and does not have one of its own

- **Power Source** – a micro USB slot for a power source of 5v

Raspberry Pi 3 is the most convenient and best model because it has the ability to connect wirelessly to the internet and to other devices using Bluetooth. This increases the mobility of the Raspberry Pi, allowing group connections and far easier use.

In the next chapter, we are going to look at setting up your Pi 3 and peripherals

Chapter 2: Setting Up Your Raspberry Pi 3

If you have just bought a brand-new Raspberry Pi 3, remove it carefully from its protective bag, which is anti-static and lace it carefully onto a flat surface that's not conductive. To use your Pi 3, you are going to need some other stuff. You will want some kind of display so that you can see what you are doing; a mouse and a keyboard as input devices, allowing you to navigate around your Pi 3 and, depending on what you are going to be doing with it, possibly some speakers and a way to connect to the internet. In this chapter, we will look at how you connect these peripheral devices and how to connect to the internet, both wired and wireless.

Connecting a Display

Before you begin to use your Pi 3, you will need a display of some kind, and the Pi 3 has support for three different types of video output – HDMI video, composite video, and DSI video. HDMI and composite are easily accessible to you while, to use DSI, you will need some special hardware. For most people, HDMI and composite are sufficient.

- ### Composite Video
Composite video can be used through the silvered and yellow port that you will see at the top of your Pi 3. This is an RCA phono connector and it is designed to connect older display devices to the Raspberry Pi 3. The connector is used to create a composite of the three colors that are common in an image – red, green, and blue. It then sends that image down a single wire to the connected

7

display, which will typically be an older monitor or a CRT (Cathode Ray Tube) television.

If this is the only device you have available to use, the composite is ideal to get you started. Don't expect great quality because you won't get it and composite connections are lacking in clarity, prone to interference and are limited in resolution.

- **HDMI Video**

You can get a much better picture quality through HDMI – High Definition Multimedia Interface. The HDMI port is the only port on the bottom of the Raspberry Pi 3 so you can't miss it. In contrast to the composite connection, which provides an analog signal, the HDMI port provides for a high-speed digital connection, giving a picture perfect in pixels, both on an HD television and on a computer monitor. If you use the HDMI port on your Pi 3, you can display full HD 1920 x 1080 resolution pictures, providing far more detail than using the composite port. If you intend to use your Pi 3 with your own computer, do make sure that the PC has an HDMI port as well. That said, it doesn't matter too much if it doesn't. the HDMI cable has a digital signal that maps to DVI – Digital Video Interface – which is a common monitor standard for computers. You can use an HDMI to DVI cable and connect your Pi to your computer in that way.

If your monitor is older and has a VGA input – the connector shaped like a D with 15 pins in blue and silver – you cannot directly connect your Pi 3 to it. Instead, you must use an adaptor dongle, specifically one that will convert HDMI to VGA and has compatibility with the Raspberry Pi 3.

- **DSI Video**

Lastly, we have DSI and this port can be found above the slot for the microSD card at the top of the circuit board – you will see a ribbon connector that is protected by a plastic layer. This port is for the Display Serial Interface which is a video standard that is commonly used in the flat panel displays on mobile devices. You will rarely find a display for sale with a DSI connector; they tend to be reserved for those who want to create compact and self-contained systems, generally engineers.

Connecting Audio

Audio is very easy if you use the HDMI port on your Pi 3, provided you configure it correctly, and it will carry both a digital audio and a video signal. This means that, with just one cable, you can get both pictures and sound. Assuming that you are going to connect your Pi 3 to a standard HDMI display, there isn't much more to do than connecting the cable!

- ## Connecting a Keyboard and Mouse

After sorting out the output peripherals for your Pi 3, its time to look at input and for that, you are going to need a keyboard and a mouse or trackball. If you already have these but they have a PS/2 connector (the round connector with the pins in a horseshoe shape) you will need to replace them with ones that have USB connections. You can buy a PS/2 adaptor but these are not satisfactory and your keyboard or mouse may not work correctly. The Pi 3 is expecting your devices to connect through USB and that is what you need to have. Depending on whether you repurchased model A or B, you will have one or two USB ports and you can connect directly to these. You may need to consider purchasing a USB hub to connect more than one device.

- ## USB Ports

It is a good investment to get a USB hub. Even with the model B, both of your ports are going to be used up with a mouse and keyboard and that leaves you none free for anything else, like an external hard drive, a joystick, storage device or optical drive, for example. You do need to buy one that is powered – the passive models may have a cheaper price tag but they are not up to the task of running external hard drives and CD drives that require a lot of power.

- **Card Reader**

If your computer or laptop does not have a built-in card reader/writer, you will need to purchase an external one. You are going to have to load the operating system onto the card before you can install it on your Raspberry Pi 3.

A Note on Storage

It probably hadn't escaped your notice that the Pi does not have a hard drive for storage; instead, it makes use of a MicroSD (Secure Digital) memory card, the kind of solid-state system for storage that you generally see in a digital camera. Most SD cards will work in the Pi but not all are equal. You need at least 4, preferably a minimum of 8 GB to hold everything you need, the operating system, files, etc. You can purchase SD cards that are pre-loaded with the Raspbian operating system directly from the Raspberry Pi store; if you have one of these, simply slot it into the SD card slot.

Connecting to a network

The Raspberry Pi 3 Model A has not onboard networking so if this what you bought you will need to purchase some extra equipment. The Model B is fully equipped with Wi-Fi and I will cover that shortly. First, let's look at how to connect the Model A to a network:

- **Networking the Model A**

So that your Model A Pi 3 has the same capabilities for networking that the Model B has, you will need to obtain a USB-adapted Ethernet adaptor. This will connect to a USB port on the Pi or on a connected USB hub and will give you a wired connection with an RJ45 connector, as you get on the Model B.

You need to purchase a 10/100 USB Ethernet adapter – these numbers refer to the speed modes – 10 MB/S and 100MB/S – and you can get these online or at an electronics retail store for very little money. Do be sure to buy an adaptor that specifies it supports the Linux operating system. There are some that will only work on Windows and these will not be compatible with the Pi. Also, don't be tempted into buying an adaptor that is gigabit-class, likely referred to as 10/100/1000. The standard USB port on the Pi 3 is not up to the job of coping with the speed that a gigabit Ethernet connection provides and you won't gain anything from it.

Wired Networking

So, to get your Model A Raspberry Pi on the network or if you want to run your Model B through wired networking, you must connect an RJ45 Ethernet patch cable to run between the Pi and a router, hub or switch. If you don't have one of these, connect your laptop or desktop to your Pi with a patch cable. There is a special cable to do this, called a crossover cable. In this type of cable, both the transmit and receive pairs are swapped, stopping the devices from talking over each other – this is the job that would normally be handled by the hub or switch.

The Pi 3 is incredibly clever, though; the RJ45 port on the Pi has a feature called Auto-MDI and this lets it automatically reconfigure itself. Because of that, you can use any type of RJ45 cable, whether it is a crossover or not, to connect your Pi to the network and it will configure itself automatically.

If you go down the route of connecting your Pi straight to your computer, you are not going to be able to connect to the internet by default. You will need to configure the computer to acts as a bridge between the wired port and another connection, usually wireless. I won't go into details in this book but you can get help by searching the Help files on your operating system for "bridge network" to get some guidance.

If you connect direct to the router, hub or switch, the Pi 3 will receive all the details that it needs to gain access to the internet when its operating system is loaded through DHCP – Dynamic Host Configuration Protocol. This will assign an IP – Internet Protocol – address to the pi in your network and it will tell it which gateway it needs to go through to access the internet, usually the IP address that your router or modem uses.

- **Wireless Networking**

You can also give your Model A Pi wireless networking capabilities by adding a wireless USB adaptor. With one of these, you can connect your Pi 3to a good range of networks including those on the 802.11n high-speed Wi-Fi standard. Before you purchase your USB adaptor, make sure of the following:

- Linux must be down as a supported operating system. Some will only support Windows and Mac OS X which means they are not compatible with the Raspberry Pi.
- Make sure that your Wi-Fi network is supported by the adapter you buy. The type of network will be shown in the specs as a number and a letter. For example, if your network is 802.11a, then a wireless adaptor for 802.11g is not going to work.
- Check the frequencies that the card supports. Some Wi-Fi standards, such as 802.11a, provide support for more than one frequency. If your adaptor is designed for a 2.4 GHz network, it will not connect to a 5 GHz network.
- Make sure you know what encryption type your network uses. Most of the modern USB adapters will support most, if not all, forms of encryption but if you go for an older or second-hand adapter, it may not connect to your Wi-Fi network. Common types of encryption include WEP, which is somewhat outdated now, WPA and WPA 2.

Configuring the connection is done in Linux so, for now, simply attach your adapter to your Pi 3, preferably through a USB hub.

Chapter 3: Setting Up Your Operating System

There are quite a few operating systems that will work on the Raspberry Pi but the main one and the one recommended for newbies is Raspbian. There are a couple of ways to get this – direct install or NOOBS – New Out Of Box Software – which can either be downloaded from the Raspberry Pi official site or you can purchase a microSD card with the software already installed. More about that later; first let's look at how to install and set up Raspbian on your Raspberry Pi 3.

How to Install Raspbian

Raspbian is the most popular operating system for the Raspberry Pi, for both newbies and for experienced users. The main reason for this is the desktop GUI, a feature that allows you find and open files, check directories and run programs without the need to input hundreds of lines of code. With the graphical user interface on the desktop, you can get into just about everything you need using a mouse and navigate through the system in exactly the same way as you do on your current desktop or mobile operating system. Here's how to download and install Raspbian OS onto your Raspberry Pi3:

- **Download Raspbian**

Open the browser on your computer and navigate to www.raspberrypi.org/downloads and look for the latest version of Raspbian. The download should be about 500 MB, somewhat larger than many of the other distributions, simply because of the GUI and the fact that this distribution is fully featured.

- **Load the RPI Installer**

You now need to install the Win32diskimager installer so, on your computer again, navigate to www.sourceforge.net/projects/win32diskimager/. Download the installer. This is going to allow you to copy the Raspbian image that you downloaded first onto your microSD card. Once the installer is downloaded, unzip the Raspbian file.

- **Choose an Image File**

Open the Disk Imager and chose which image you want to copy over to the card. To do this, look for the folder icon located above the Image File option and open it. Select the image and click OK.

- **Choose the microSD card**

Now click on Device Menu and pick which SD card you want to load the image onto. Before you do, make sure that your card has been formatted in the FAT32 format as this is the only format that Raspberry Pi will recognize. And make sure that, if you have anything on the card that you save it to your computer – once you select the card to copy the Raspbian image to, any data that is on that card will be permanently wiped off. Once you are happy that you have done everything, and that you are loading the image to the right card, click on Write.

- **Wait for the Writing Process to Complete**

Now the process of writing the image to the microSD card will start and your chosen image will be copied over. The length of time it takes to copy will depend on your SD card, the speed of it but usually it will take a few minutes. If things don't seem to be working, start over but, this time, right click on the icon for Win 32 Disk Imager and click on Run as Administrator.

- **Boot the operating System Up**

When the process has successfully completed, safely eject the SD card from your computer and then insert it into the slot on your Pi 3. Switch your Pi on and you will see a Setup menu. There are already many default values set so just hit the Enter key on your keyboard and keep pressing it until you come to the Command Prompt. Here, type the command startx and press the Enter key again. The Raspbian GUI will now load.

Using Raspbian for the First Time

Now that Raspbian is loaded, you will go straight to the Software Configuration Tool – this will happen automatically. This tool may be called Raspi-config, depending on which distribution you are using. For the purposes of this, we will use Raspi-config. This menu is where you make changes to some settings on your Raspberry Pi 3. Do be aware that you will not be able to use a mouse while you are doing this, not the first time anyway. To go through each of the options you will need to use the arrow keys that are on the keyboard or you can use the Tab key. Press the Enter key to confirm each of your choices and then wait for the net menu to load.

The following options will be visible in the Raspi-config menu:

- **Expand Filesystem**
If you used a NOOBS card to install Raspbian, you can skip over this option as all the space on your card is available for use. If you used the image option detailed above, you must select this option to make the best use of your SD card when you launch the Raspberry Pi 3 for the first time.

- **Change the User Password**
As you should do with anything that has a default user password, for security reasons, you should change it to a new one. The default user password is "pi" so select this option and type in a new password – you do this at the bottom of the screen and then you must type it again to confirm it.

- **Enable Boot to Desktop**
  Internationalization Options

- **Change Locale**

If you are content to use English as your language, leave this setting, otherwise change it to the one you want.

- **Change Time Zone**
Raspberry Pi 3 is able to automatically detect what time zone you are in when you connect up to the internet. However, you must select the option now to make sure that your settings are right for the date and time. Pick the region you are in and then select the city that is the nearest to your time zone.

- **Change Your Keyboard Layout**
Select this option and a list of keyboard models will appear. Pick yours from the list – if you don't see it, pick a generic setting so that the symbols you use on your desktop or mobile operating system are available to you.

You can also set Compose Key, allowing you to use characters that are not normally on the keyboard and you can set the shortcut option of CTRL+Alt+Backspace – this will let you quickly shut X Server down.

Enable Camera

Select this option if you want to be able to toggle and externally attached camera on and off.

Add to Rastrack

Rastrack is a program that tracks all Pi 3s are across the entire globe so if you want yours mapped select this option. This will allow you to communicate with other users and will let them know where your Pi 3 is located. If you wanted to change the location of your Pi 3, remove any information that you have shared on Rastrack or make changes to your user details, you can go to www.rastrack.co.uk.

Overclock

When you overclock, you tweak the configuration in ways that are not quite what the manufacturer intended, to make things move faster. When you choose this option, you will see a menu telling you that overclocking may affect the lifespan of the Pi 3. If you know what you are doing, you can change the settings without adversely affecting your Pi 3 lifespan. If you are not confident, do not touch these settings. There are some presets that you cannot change if your power supply and configuration are not right. If you are not able to use the setting that you want, you will need to press down on the SHIFT key – this will disable the option for overclocking.

Advanced Options

- **Overscan**
  This allows you to set the size of the border around the screen image. If you find that your monitor is causing overspill, you should set the image so it is to the right.

- **Hostname**
  This option will let you make changes to your Raspberry Pi 3 name, the one that shows up on other devices on the same network. Your Pi 3 has a default name and that is raspberrypi. There is no need to change this, unless you want to or unless you have a more than one Raspberry Pi attached to your network.

- **L memory_split**
  The memory on your Raspberry Pi 3 is split between the GPU and the CPU and both of these are responsible for running different programs. Some of these programs will need more of the GPU than the CPU and others will need more CPU. If you select this option, you can improve your Raspberry Pi 3 performance by providing the larger share of the memory to the necessary processor

- **SSH**
  By selecting this option, you can create a secure connection between your devices and computers. This is so that can control one device from another, remotely and if you select this option you can enable or disable that.

- **SPI**

The Raspberry Pi 3 will communicate with devices that are connected as add-ons to the same board through the SPI kernel. Choosing this setting will make it simple to add other circuits, like sensors, to your board.

- **Audio**

If you find that your audio is not loud enough, choose this option to force the sound out of the jack or HDMI

- **Update**

This setting will allow Raspi-config to update whenever a new update is available for it. For this to work, your Pi 3 must be connected to the internet.

When you have finished making your changes, press the Right arrow on your keyboard until you get to the option for Finish and then hit the Enter key. You might be required to restart the Pi 3 so that the changes will be put in place but that will be dependent on what changes have been made.

If you want to start Raspi-config at any time, simply type the following command in at the command prompt:

sudo raspi-config

Important

If you download the Jessie distribution of Raspbian, you may not see Raspi-config. Jessie distribution lets you use a relegation of it and that means you don't need to type in the above command. Instead, the configuration can be accessed directly from the graphical user interface by clicking on the Menu option in the toolbar and then clicking on Preferences and Raspberry Pi Configuration Tool. The options that appear will be separated into categories under four tabs and this is what you will see:

System

- Auto login

- Boot options (choice between command line interface or desktop)
- Change hostname
- Change Password
- Expand Filesystem
- Overscan
- Rastrack

Interfaces

- Camera
- I2C
- Serial
- SPI
- SSH

Performance

- Overclock
- GPU Memory

Localization

- Set Keyboard
- Set Locale
- Set Time zone

Once the changes you desire have been made, you will need to restart your operating system so that the changes are recognized. Click Yes and your Pi 3 will reboot.

Logging in for the First Time

When you first turn the Pi 3 on, you will be asked for our username and your password. Until you change them, the default settings are "pi" for username and "raspberry" for the password – they are both case sensitive. You will not see any screen feedback when you type the password in like you do on the desktop or mobile operating system, but this is a security thing as it masks any key activity. When you have input your password, hit the Enter key.

When you have logged in successfully and opted to boot from CLI, you will see the command line prompt and it will have the following line showing:

pi@raspberrypi ~ $

Now you can begin managing your Pi 3 and all your files and programs.

Next, we are going to look at installing from NOOBS.

NOOBS

NOOBS stands for New Out Of Box Software and it is an easy way to get Raspbian onto your Pi 3. You can do this in one of two ways – either purchase a microSD card that is preinstalled or download NOOBS onto your SD card and install it to your Pi 3. The first way is self-explanatory when you insert the card so we are going to look at installing NOOBS onto your SD card.

Download NOOBS to Your Computer

Open your computer browser and go to www.raspberrypi.org/downloads. Choose the latest version and download it – be aware that this is a big file and it will take time to successfully download. If you are on a capped internet system and only allowed 1 GB per month, you are not going to be able to download this. If this is the case for you, you will need to buy a preinstalled card.

To successfully download NOOBS onto your card, the SD card must be a minimum of 4 GB, higher is better if you intend to install other software and applications onto it.

Download NOOBS to Your SD Card

Before you go any further, you need to make sure your card is formatted to FAT32. If this is a brand-new card, you don't need to do this but if you have used it with other devices, this is a necessary step:

How to Format Your SD Card as FAT32

This will only work for cards of 32GB or lower.

Windows:

- Download the Formatting tool from www.sdcard.org
- In the options menu, you must set FORMAT SIZE ADJUSTMENT to On to make sure that the whole card is formatted and not just a partition. Once the format is complete, you will see the updated size.

Mac OS

You can use the Formatting tool listed above for Mac OS but you can also use the OS X Disk Utility that comes with Mac OS X. DO be careful that you choose the SD card to format and not your entire hard disk! Go into the utility and select the correct SD card volume and then select Erase with MS-DOS format.

Linux

Linux users should use gparted or parted (command line version) and you can find full instructions www.qdosmsq.dunbar-it.co.uk/blog/2013/06/noobs-for-raspberry-pi

Once your card is formatted, download the NOOBS files from www.raspberrypi.org/downloads. Extract the files and then insert the card into your card reader. Copy the files you extracted onto the card making sure that the file is at the root directory on the card. If the files get extracted to a folder, simply open the folder and copy the files to the root. Eject the card safely and insert it into your Pi 3.

When you boot up for the first time, the FAT partition on your card called RECOVERY will automatically change size to the minimum and a list of the operating systems on the card will be displayed. There are several preinstalled systems but the best one is Raspbian and that is what we are using.

Chapter 4: Installing Software on Raspberry Pi 3

Compared to other boards of its kind, the Raspberry Pi is the best for learning and that is down to the fact that it is so flexible, and its operating system is compatible cross-platform. However, to implement any computing or gaming projects, be it an Android emulation or a media center, you need to understand how to install software that can run on the computer.

You could install another operating system if you wanted, software that comes from the Raspberry Pi store or that comes from another repository. To be fair, to install software on the Raspberry Pi 3 is as simple as installing the software of your choice on your computer or mobile device. However, if you are new to Linux, it will all look unfamiliar to you to start with; learning it is simple and you will soon pick it up. We already talked about installing the operating system on your Pi 3 and, once that has been done, you can begin to install the software you want. The easiest way to do this is through the command line.

Let us assume that you have decided to install the tool called Scrot. To do that, you would type the following line at the command prompt:

Sudo apt-get install scrot

To search through all the available repositories for the software we want, we use the apt-get install syntax. This identifies the right files and downloads them.

Raspberry Pi Store

As it is a unique product, Linux stands out from all the rest and the developers have worked hard at finding ways to make it much easier to use. As a result, there are several different distributions, like Ubuntu and Mint and both of these make life easier when it comes to installing software into the Pi 3.

For a start, the package manager is very much like the search engines you use on your desktop operating system, in that it will filter the results to ensure the right applications or software are found. Most of the available software repositories can be found in certain Linux distributions, similar to the command line on a mouse-driven user interface.

Secondly, you can also find software and applications in app stores and it just so happens that Raspberry Pi has its own dedicated store. To download the software and install it from either option, open the command prompt and type in the following command:

Sudo apt-get update && sudo apt-get install pistore

Just like when you download and install any software to your computer, a new icon will show up on the desktop when the installation is complete. To open it, double-click on the icon and a window will appear. This shows all the applications that you can download and, just like the Google Play Store or iOS App Store, the applications are shown in lists with screenshots and technical information.

Again, very much like installing to your mobile or computer, it is very straightforward to download an app from the Raspberry Pi store. Sign in or create an account if you don't already have one and then search for what you are looking for. When you find the app you want, simply click on Install and then choose from one of several payment methods. Once you have successfully made the payment, the application will install. Unlike other stores, because the Pi is smaller and has less RAM available, you can only install apps one at a time. Most of the software that is user-generated will be cheap or free.

That's the easy part; the hard part is in learning which commands to use and where to use them to be certain the installation will be successful. Although t can sometimes be a challenge, Raspberry Pi was designed to help people learn how to code and in the next couple of chapters we will be looking at basic Linux commands and coding with Python.

There are also lots of forums and websites where you can get information and help, not just about the Pi but about coding as well. And, to make life even easier, you can have Raspberry Pi store on your desktop so you can easily see if there are any application updates.

Chapter 5: Raspberry Pi 3 and Linux

Although you can choose from any of hundreds of different distributions of Linux, each of them shares one set of common tools and these are called commands. They are operated in the terminal, at the command prompt and are pretty much the same as those used on Mac OS and Windows. However, to be successful with your Raspberry Pi 3, there are a series of basic Linux commands that you must learn first:

- **ls -** a shortened version of list, ls will give you the contents of the directory you are in at the time you use it. You can also call it listing the directory as an argument. An example would by to type ls/home at the command prompt; this will give you a list of what is in home, no matter what directory you are in at the time. The Windows version of this command is dir.

- **cd** – a shortened version of change directory. This allows you to find your way through the file system. If you just type cd at the prompt, you will be taken straight back to the home directory. If you type cd/ followed by the name of the directory that you want to go to, you will be taken to the specified directory. Be aware that a directory can be relative or it can be absolute. For example, typing cd boot will take you to the directory under your current directory called boot but typing in cd/boot will take you to the boot directory no matter where you are.

- **mv** – this is the move command and, in Linux, it has two purposes. First, it lets you move a file from one directory over to another and it will also let you rename a directory. That last feature might seem a little odd but, in terms of Linux, what you are doing is moving the file from one name over to another. The command we use is named my oldfile e newfil e.

- **rm** - shortened version of remove, this will delete files. Whatever you type after the command, be it a single file or a list of files will be deleted. The Windows equivalent of this is del and both commands share a common requirement – that you ensure the correct file or files is deleted because this cannot be undone

- **rmdir** – shortened version of remove directory. On its own, rm cannot normally remove a directory, only files contained within the directories. Because of this, rmdir is used to delete the directory once rm has been used to empty it of files.

- **mkdir** – the shortened version of make directory, mkdir is the polar opposite of rmdir. If you were to type in mkdir myfolder at the command prompt, a new directory named myfolder would be created under the working directory you are in. as with the cd command, any directory that is given to the command may be relative or absolute.

Linux System Administration

Linux is a multi-user operating system that lets several users log in and use the same computer. To ensure that each user's privacy is kept safe and to keep the computer itself safe, each user's abilities are restricted.

Most users will be able to run virtually all programs and will be able to edit and save folders that are stored in their own home folder. Normal users are not able to edit the files that are stored in any other user's folder, nor can they touch the system files. The only person in Linux who can do this is known as the superuser and that user has the username of root. The superuser is not restricted in anything and can do pretty much what is needed.

Sudo Command

You would not usually log in as root on the computer but there is a command that gives the superuser access – the sudo command. If you were to log into your Pi 3 as pi user, you would be logged in as a normal user. To run commands as the root user, you would use the sudo command in front of any programs that you wanted to run.

For example, let's say that you want to install some software onto Raspbian; normally you would use the tool called apt-get. If you want to update the list of software available, you would need to add the sudo command in front, like this:

sudo apt-get update

You can also use the command, sudo su, to run a superuser shell. When you run a command as a superuser, however, there is nothing standing in the way of you making mistakes that could irrevocably damage the system so do be careful and only run as a superuser when it is absolutely necessary – make sure that, when you are done, you come out of the superuser shell and go back to being a normal user.

Who Is Able to Use Sudo?

It would go against the whole idea of security is just anyone could use the sudo command to log in as a superuser. To that end, users must be approved as superusers to gain the administrator privileges that go with the sudo command. The pi user is automatically included in the approved user list and, to let others use sudo, you must add them to the sudo group. There ae three ways to do this:

- with usermod command
- with the visudo command
- by editing the /etc/sudoers file

All user management is carried out on the command line in Raspbian. The default user will be pi with a password of raspberry and you can add new users and change the passwords of all users.

Changing Your Password

If you are logged in as pi, you would use the command passwd to change your password:

- Type passwd at the command prompt and press the Enter key
- You will be asked to input the current password as a way of authenticating who you are.
- Next, you will be asked to input your new password so type it in and press the Enter key
- Now confirm your password by typing it in again and note, as we said before, you will not see any input on the screen as you type it in.
- Once your password has been successfully confirmed you will see a message that says "passwd: password updated successfully". Your new password will come into force straight away

If the user does have sudo permission, they can change the password of another user and this is done by typing in passwd and the users name. For example, typing in sudo passwd bella will let you change the password for bella and a few other optional values for that user, such as their name. Press Enter to skip over each option.

To remove a password, you would type in sudo passwd, followed by the user's name and d; for example, sudo passwd bella -d.

Managing Users

To create a new user, simply type in sudo adduser and the name of the user. You will be asked for their password but, if you don't want to add one, just leave it blank.

When a new user has been created, they will get their own folder in the home directory. The piusers folder is located at /home/pi/.

When the user is created, /etc/skel/ contents are copied to the home folder for the new user. You can add or modify any dot-file, like .bash/rc. in /etc/skel as you want them and the new version will then be applied across the board to all users.

Sudoers

Default pi users are automatically sudoers on Raspbian and they have the ability to use the sudo command to run commands as root and also to use the command sudo su to switch over to the root user. To add new users to sudoers, the command to be run, by a sudoer user, is sudo visudo. Then you must look under the commented header, # User privilege specification and find the line that says ALL= (ALL: ALL) ALL.

Copy that line that change from root to username. To allow root access without a password, you should change it to NOPASSWD: ALL. The following example is providing bella with sudo access with no password:

User privilege specification

root ALL= (ALL: ALL) ALL

bella ALL = NOPASSWD: ALL

Save the changes and then exit to apply them but do be careful; it is wholly possible to delete your own rights to use sudo by accident.

The editor that the visudo command uses is Nano by default and to change that, you would type in

update-alternatives --set editor /usr/bin/vim.tiny

Thus, setting the editor as Vim.

How to Delete a User

Users on the system can be deleted through the command userdel. If you also wanted to remove their home folder, you would add the -r flag, like this:

sudo userdel -r bella

This removes the user called Bella and her home folder.

That covers the basics of Linux so next, we will look at how to code in Raspbian using Python.

Chapter 6: Raspberry Pi 3 and Python

You don't just have one programming language to use with the Raspberry Pi 3; there are many to choose from and the primary one is Python. Not only is it easy to learn and use, it is fully compatible with the Linux operating system.

Just like how the Pi was originally designed as a teaching tool, so Python was originally designed as a teaching language which makes them the perfect fit for one another. The syntax used in Python is incredibly easy to learn, it is straightforward and is not complicated at all. And, like the Raspbian operating system, Python is also a cross-platform language. Because of this, the number of commands and instructions have been reduced compared to many of the other languages and has since surged in popularity for both applications and embedded systems.

To successfully program the Raspberry Pi 3, you must first have a firm grasp on the basics of Python and how to program with it. If you are already a computer programmer that uses Python, you can skip over this chapter if you want. We will look at the concepts involved in Python programming as well as a brief look at what it's all about.

Overview of Programming with Python

- Out of all the computer programming languages, Python is the easiest to use and the easiest to learn. This is because the syntax is simple and all the code you write gets compiled at runtime, unlike other languages. That means, before the code is executed, you will be informed of any errors, giving you the chance to put them right.

- Python language is interactive and you can use it in the development of any situation where a question is asked, with the answers being processed and then prompted in the output of the code.
- Python is the best language for beginners to learn and for those who are new to the concept of programming. Python has many uses including a lot of web applications and simple text processing tasks.
- Python is known as object-oriented programming, or OOP for short. All outputs are real time applications and many of the concepts come from C++.

As I said earlier, Python works cross-platform and you can install it on any of these platforms:

- Windows CE

- OS/2

- DOS

- VMS/OpenVMS

- Psion

- VxWorks

- PalmOS

- UNIX systems (Solaris, Linux, FreeBSD, AIX, HP/UX, SunOS, IRIX, etc.)

- Acorn/RISC OS

- BeOS

- Macintosh (Intel, PPC, 68K)

- Amiga

- QNX

- Nokia mobile

- Java and .NET virtual machines

- Basic Syntax

- Win 9x/NT/2000/XP/Vista/7/8/10

There are two types of programming in Python:

- **Interactive Mode** – this involves you passing commands that invoke the interpreter. The interpreter will read the commands and respond to any instructions given within it. For example, typing in this:

```
Print ('Hello, Python!');
```

Would be output on your screen as:

```
>> Hello, Python!
```

- **Script Mode** – this involves you using a script parameter as a way of trying to invoke the interpreter. The parameter will begin executing the script from start to finish. For example, let's assume that the interpreter already knows and can see the path that leads to the script, along with the file that is going to be executed; we could input this:

```
$ python test.py
```

And the output would be:

```
Hello, Python!
```

Python Concepts

There are two main concepts that we will be looking at:

- **Python Identifiers** – these are words that are user-defined and can be used as classes, variables, functions, constants, or modules. Identifiers can contain the following characters – A to Z, a to z, 0 to 9 and underscores (_). If you use any other special character, the result will be an error.
- **Reserved Words** – Like most computer programming languages, Python has a number of reserved keywords. These can only be used for specific tasks and functions and may not be used in naming or as identifiers. For example, the "print" command is a reserved keyword; you cannot use it anywhere else.

All keywords must be written in lower case and this is the list of those in Python:

- yield
- with
- while
- try
- return
- raise
- print
- pass
- or
- not
- lambda
- is
- in
- import
- if
- global
- from
- for

- finally
- exec
- except
- else
- elif
- del
- def
- continue
- class
- break
- assert
- and

Basic Python Operators

We use Python operators to do basic mathematical and logical operations based on user input; the generated output is logic. The following is a list of all the operators in Python:

- Arithmetic

- Assignment

- Bitwise

- Comparison (Relational)

- Identity

- Logical

- Membership

Arithmetic:

The arithmetic operators are used to carry out basic arithmetic, where math calculations are needed. They are as follows:

Arithmetic operators perform basic arithmetic and are used where math calculation is required:

- Addition (+)
- Division (/)
- Exponent (**)
- Modulus (%) – this will provide the remainder after the division of two terms
- Multiplication (*)
- Subtraction (-)

Assignment:

The assignment operators are used when we need logical or arithmetic equations. They are as follows:

- = - used to assign a value to a variable
- += - used to add the right-side operand and to add a value to the left side operand
- -= or *= - is used in the same way as the one above

Bitwise:

We use bitwise operators for tasks where binary numbers are used, for example:

- A: 0 0 0 1 1 1 1 0
- B: 1 1 0 0 0 0 1 1
-
- _____
- A&B: 0 0 0 0 0 0 1 0
- A|B: 1 1 0 1 1 1 1 1

- `A^B: 1 1 0 1 1 1 0 1`
- `~A: 1 1 1 0 0 0 0 1`

Comparison:

We use the comparison operators to help us to compare quantities; the output is based on what the observation is. These are the comparison operators:

- != - not equal to
- <= - less than or equal to
- == - equal to
- >= - greater than or equal to

Identity:

The identity operators are used when was need to identify if a statement holds credibility or not. This is done by assigning the operator "is" to a statement where the left and right operands are both pointing to the same object. The output will be TRUE but, if the operands do not point the same object, the output would be FALSE. The 'is not" operator is used when we want to check that the left and right operands do not point to the same object. The output would be TRUE if they didn't but, if they did the output would be FALSE.

Logical:

Logical operators are used when we want basic tasks performed, such as:

- OR – where one condition is true, like A or B
- NOT – where the output will be the opposite of input
- AND – where both conditions are true, like A and B

Membership:

We use the membership operators to test for membership in a sequence, like a tuple, list or string:

- in – this will check the sequence for membership; if it is found the output will be TRUE; if it is not found, the output will be FALSE.
- not in – this will check to see if a specific character is present. If it is, the output will be TRUE; if it isn't, the output will be FALSE.

Sample program:

This program was specifically written for the Pi and is used as a way of programming the GPIO pins that are available on the Pi board; the program is assigned to a function:

```
#blink.py //this will open the file where the
instructions are stored

Import RPi.GPIO as GPIO //this will set the
default instructions to make sure the GPIO port is
included

Import time //this is used to keep time

GPIO.setmode(GPIO.BOARD)

GPIO.setup(7, GPIO.OUT)

While true:

GPIO.output

(7, True)

Time.sleep(0.2)

GPIO.output(7, False)

Time.sleep (0.2)
```

This program was written to make the LED lights on the board blink on and off. As you can see from the program, we initialized GPIO pin 7. A While loop is started and, when the logic that is contained in "blink.py" becomes true, the loop begins iterating and will continue to do so until false is reached. In this loop provided the logic for GPIO pin 7 is true, the LED lights are switched on and will stay on for 0.2 seconds. When it reaches false, these lights turn off for 0.2 seconds. This loop will continue to be iterated the Pi 3 is turned off. This is because there is no false condition included that will stop the loop from iterating.

Fixing Common Python Errors

While Python is one of the most user-friendly languages, it can still be challenging to those new to programming. You will come up against errors and most of these are common so let's have a look at what you might come up against and how you can fix them:

- **Getting expressions and defaults confused for function-based arguments**

Python gives you a way of identifying when a function argument is an option because it provides it with a default value. While this is a useful feature, it can cause confusion, particularly when the default value remains mutable. Have a look at this example of a Python function definition:

```
>>>    def   foo(   bar=[    ]    )    :
            # bar is an option and defaults to [ ]
if it isn't specified

      .    .    .    bar.append    ("baz"   )
            # this line could cause a problem, as
you may be able to see

   . . . return bar
```

So, what error are we looking at? You must not make the mistake of thinking that an optional argument will automatically match a default expression when a function is used without giving it an optional argument value. In this example, we could have assumed that, because we called foo(), we would get 'baz' returned automatically because, when foo() is used, bar is automatically set as[]. In the next example, we can see what would happen if this was done:

```
>>> foo ( )

[ "baz" ]

>>> foo ( )

[ "baz" , "baz" ]

>>> foo ( )

[ "baz" , "baz" , "baz" ]
```

Did you notice that the default value of "baz" kept on changing to the existing line whenever foo() was used, instead of going to a new list? When you get more advanced in Python programming, you will learn that any default value associate with function arguments are calculated once and only once – at the time the function is defined. That means that the argument called bar is initialized to its own default value but foo() has to be defined first. This will mean that any other foo() calls will be used in the same list as bar was initialized in. The following example shows you the fix for this:

```
>>> def foo (bar=None ) :

. . . if bar is None;

. . . bar = [ ]
```

```
. . . bar.append( "baz" )
. . . return bar
. . .
>>> foo ( )
[ "baz" ]
>>> foo ( )
[ "baz" ]
>>> foo ( )
[ "baz" ]
```

- ## Using Class Variables The Wrong Way

```
>>> class A(object) :
. . . x = 1
. . .
>>> class B(A) :
. . . pass
. . .
>>> class C(A) :
. . . pass
. . .
>>> print A.x, B.x, C.x
1 1 1
```

This code makes some kind of sense as a starting point but let's take it a bit further:

```
>>> B.x = 2
>>>print A.x, B.x, C.x
1 2 1
```

This is also correct:

```
>>> A.x = 3
>>> print A.x, B.x, C.x
3 2 3
```

Wait there! What happened here? A.x was meant to be the only one that changed so why did C.x change? In Python, variables are handled internally as dictionaries and, as such, abide by the Method Resolution Order (MRO). In the code above, attribute x has not been put into class C and that means the only classes that will look it up are the base classes. In this example, that base class is A. This means that C has no x property and when C.x is referenced, it goes directly to A.x

- **Ensure You Are Using The Correct Parameters**

```
>>> try :
...             1 = [ "a" , "b" }
...             int (1[2])
```

```
.   .   .                    except    ValueError,
IndexError:              #  To  catch  both  of  the
exceptions, right

.  .  .                 pass

.  .  .

Traceback                 (the   most   recent   call
last) :

File  "<stdin>" , line 3, in <module>

IndexError : list index out of range
```

Did you spot the error? We don't have any of exceptions that have been properly specified inside our except statement. E is meant to connect that exception with what has been specified as parameter number two. In our example, e is parameter 2 and that means it is available for any inspection needed and the result of this is the IndexError exception not being used as it should be by the except statement. Instead it has been bound to the parameter called IndexError.

There is a correct way to use multiple exceptions inside except statements and that is to ensure that the parameter has been specified as being a tuple, with all exceptions that will be caught. It is also best practice to make use of the keyword "as" because that is universal syntax.

```
>>> try:

.  .  .                 1 = ["a , "b"]

.  .  .                 int (1[2])

.  .  .                 except (ValueError, IndexError)
as e:
```

```
. . .                    pass

. . .

>>>
```

- **Not Understanding the Scope Rules in Python**

Scope in Python is based on the Local, Enclosing, Global, Built-In rule (LEGB rule). If you are used to Python, this will be straightforward but there are quite a few things that can throw up errors. This is a common Python code that has the scope to cause problems:

```
>>> x = 10

>>> def foo():

...      x += 1

...      print x

...

>>> foo()

Traceback (the most recent call last):

   File "<stdin>", line 1, in <module>

   File "<stdin>", line 2, in foo

UnboundLocalError:  local   variable   'x'   is
referenced before assignment
```

The error occurs when you assign a variable that is within a scope. Python automatically assumes that that assignment is local to that scope and it then shadows all other variables that are named the same. You might not realize this and will be surprised to get the UnboundLocalError in code that has always worked before. The reason is the addition of the assigned statement into the body of the function. The same thing can happen when lists are involved:

```
>>> lst = [1, 2, 3]
>>> def foo1():
...     lst.append(5)   # This works fine...
...
>>> foo1()
>>> lst
[1, 2, 3, 5]


>>> lst = [1, 2, 3]
>>> def foo2():
...     lst += [5]      # ... but this really
doesn't!
...
>>> foo2()
Traceback (the most recent call last):
   File "<stdin>", line 1, in <module>
   File "<stdin>", line 2, in foo
UnboundLocalError: local variable 'lst' referenced
before assignment
```

While foo1 can run the way it should do, foo2 cannot. The reason is the same as in the first example and, in this case, while we haven't connected foo1 to the assignment for lst, foo2 is. You need to keep in mind that lsr+=[f5] is exactly the same as lst=lst+[5]. This attempts to assign lst a value but as the value is actually based on lst, Python assumes to be of local scope, even though it has not been defined.

- **Changing Lists and Iteration**

```
>>> odd = lambda x : bool(x % 2)

>>> numbers = [n for n in range(10)]

>>> for i in range(len(numbers)):

...        if odd(numbers[i]):

...            del numbers[i]   # BAD: Deleting an
item from the list while iterating over it

...

Traceback (most recent call last):

            File "<stdin>", line 2, in
<module>

    IndexError: list index is out of range
```

Those experienced at Python programming will be ware that, when items are deleted from arrays or lists while iteration is being done, problems will occur. The last example shows you a very clear mistake but it isn't always easy to spot ad even experienced developers will miss it.

Python makes use of several paradigms for streamlining and simplifying code and one of the biggest upsides to simple code is a lower chance of errors. List Comprehension paradigm is used to avoid the problem in the last code example:

```
>>> odd = lambda x : bool(x % 2)

>>> numbers = [n for n in range(10)]

>>> numbers[:] = [n for n in numbers if not
odd(n)]   # ahh, doesn't that look better

>>> numbers

[0, 2, 4, 6, 8]
```

- **Misunderstanding Closure Binding in Python**:

```
>>> def create_multipliers():

...        return [lambda x : i * x for i in
range(5)]

>>> for multiplier in create_multipliers():

...        print multiplier(2)

...
```

You would think that this would be the result:

```
0

2
```

4

6

8

But this is what you see instead:

8

8

8

8

8

Why did this happen? Because Python features late binding behavior. Variable values that are in a closure will be looked up when the inner function is being called. Each time a returned function is called, the value i will be in the scope that surrounds it. Some people think that a hack is the only way to get around this but here is the proper solution:

```
>>> def create_multipliers():

...         return [lambda x, i=i : i * x for i in range(5)]

...

>>> for multiplier in create_multipliers():

...         print multiplier(2)
```

```
...

0

2

4

6

8
```

We use default arguments to create anonymous functions in your favor

- **Circular Module Dependencies**

In this example, we have files named a.py and b.py; both will import the other:

```
In a.py :

import b

def f():

    return b.x

print f()

In b.py:

import a

x = 1

def g():

    print a.f()

First attempt at importing a.py:
```

```
>>> import a

1
```

That works well because we have the correct circular import in place. This isn't too much of a problem because Python already knows that it mustn't import something twice. However, it does depend on where the module is attempting to access the defined variables and functions and that is where we get the problems. In the last example, a.py imported b.py easily because b.py didn't need anything from a.py at the time of import. However, we only have one reference to b.py and that is in a.f(), defined to g(), meaning there really isn't any reason why a.py or b.py would need to invoke g().

The next example shows what happens when you attempt to import b.py:

```
>>> import b

Traceback (most recent call last):
                File "<stdin>", line 1, in
<module>

                File "b.py", line 1, in
<module>

        import a

                File "a.py", line 6, in
<module>

        print f()

          File "a.py", line 4, in f
```

```
      return b.x
```

```
   AttributeError: 'module' object has no attribute
'x'
```

This simply cannot work; while you are attempting to import b.py, Python is calling f() to import a.py and f() tries to access b.x which hasn't been defined as it should have been. The easiest way around this is get b.py to import a.py through g():

```
   x = 1



   def g():

           import a              #  This  will  be
   evaluated only when g() is called

           print a.f()
```

This time, it all works:

```
   >>> import b

   >>> b.g()

   1                   # Printed  a  first  time  because
   module 'a' calls 'print f()' at the end

   1                   # Printed  a  second  time, this is
   our call to 'g'
```

- **Clashing Names with Library Modules**

One of the best things about Python is that it comes with a lot of library modules but, for those not experienced or those not keeping their eyes open, name clashing between library modules and your own modules can occur. Some quite complex issues can arise from this because Python is attempting to import a separate library and will wind up importing the Python version. It won't know which one is needed so do take care when you are picking your names.

- **Python 2 and Python 3**

Some coders prefer Python 2 while others think Python 3 is better. If you don't know what the difference is between them, expect to see some problems arising.

```
import sys

def bar(i):

    if i == 1:

        raise KeyError(1)

    if i == 2:

        raise ValueError(2)

def bad():

    e = None

    try:

        bar(int(sys.argv[1]))

    except KeyError as e:

        print('key error')

    except ValueError as e:
```

```
      print('value error')

   print(e)

bad()
```

This will run correctly in Python 2:

```
$ python foo.py 1

key error

1

$ python foo.py 2

value error

2
```

But try it Python 3 and this is what will happen:

```
$ python3 foo.py 1

key error

Traceback (most recent call last):
  File "foo.py", line 19, in <module>
    bad()
  File "foo.py", line 17, in bad
    print(e)
UnboundLocalError: local variable 'e' referenced
before assignment
```

The reason why this code is not working in Python 3 is because, in v3, we are able to go outside the except block scope to access the exception object. To stop this from happening, make sure that you properly refer to the object outside the scope so that it is still accessible. If we were to apply that to the last example, we would find that the code can now be accessed in both versions of Python:

```
import sys

def bar(i):

    if i == 1:

        raise KeyError(1)

    if i == 2:

        raise ValueError(2)

def good():

    exception = None

    try:

        bar(int(sys.argv[1]))

    except KeyError as e:

        exception = e

        print('key error')

    except ValueError as e:

        exception = e

        print('value error')

    print(exception)

good()
```

- **Using the _del_ Method Incorrectly**

Let's assume that, in mod.py, we have this code:

```
import foo

class Bar(object):

                    . . .

    def __del__(self):

        foo.cleanup(self.myhandle)
```

Next, we will assume that you attempted this from a file called _mod.py:

```
import mod

mybar = mod.Bar()
```

This will give you an AttributeError exception because, when the interpreter shuts down, the global variables are all set to None. When _del_ is used, foo will already be set to None and the solution is to use atexit.register() because, when the program has finished executing, all of the registered handlers will be kicked out before the interpreter will close. The solution looks like this:

```
import foo

import atexit
```

```
def cleanup(handle):

    foo.cleanup(handle)

class Bar(object):

    def __init__(self):

        ...

        atexit.register(cleanup, self.myhandle)
```

by including atexit.register(), you are making the best use of the cleanup function so that the program can terminate as it should. foo.cleanup would have to make the decision on what is done with the object called self.myHandle so you need to make sure it is set up right.

You need a good grasp of Python but, when you begin using your Raspberry Pi 3, you are going to see errors and you are going to come up against several stumbling blocks. Some will be simple to fix while others won't. Sometimes it will be obvious what is wrong, sometimes it won't. Use the internet because there is always help available and always a solution.

In the next chapter, we will look at a few projects that you can do, some simple, some more complex.

Chapter 7: Raspberry Pi 3 Projects

Now you have some knowledge of your Pi 3, let's look at some of the projects you can do with it. The ones I have given the instructions for here are simple but I will also be providing links to other, more complex projects that you can have a go at:

Raspberry Pi XBMC

XBMC is the most popular of all media streaming centers and it is dead easy to get it onto your Raspberry Pi 3. You will need some extra materials:

- Raspberry Pi 3
- 3.5mm stereo audio cable – optional – only needed if your video output is analog and you require externa speakers or are going to use the speakers on your TV. If you opt of r HDMI, you won't need this cable
- Card reader (external or use the one built-in to your computer if present)
- Ethernet cable
- HDMI video cable (or composite, your choice)
- Micro USB power supply – 5V 2A is best
- Minimum 8 GB Class 10 microSD card
- Raspberry Pi case – this is optional but it will protect your Pi 3
- Raspbmc Installer – for getting the right version of XBMC for Raspberry Pi 3 onto your card. You could use OSMC if you prefer.

- Remote control, only of you don't intend using your mouse and keyboard for controlling your media center
- USB Hard drive – an optional extra, for use in storing video if you prefer not to stream from another PC
- USB mouse and keyboard

XBMC is incredibly powerful as a media center and the Pi 3 is the best choice for running it on but, you need to be aware that there are a few things that it cannot do. For a start, it cannot stream any content that comes via the internet and you won't get perfect video at 1080p. that said 720p is fine and much of what you get is going to depend on where the audio is played from – it is better to stream from a USB drive than it is the network.

Some of the menus will likely be slower and don't expect brilliant skins because you won't get them. However, it is perfectly adequate as a backup media center so let's get own with building it.

Step 1 - Install Raspbmc

This is the very first step and we are going to put it on your microSD card. This is how it's done in Windows:

- Put the microSD into your card reader
- Download the installer from www.osmc.tv and save it to your desktop.
- Run it by double-clicking the icon
- Download the files to your card and then use the safe eject feature on your computer to remove the card.

Step 2 – Hook up your Raspberry Pi 3 and install Raspbmc

Next, we need to connect the Pi 3 to the television so plug in the HDMI cable to the Pi 3 and connect it to the TV. Insert the Ethernet cable and connect it to your router and then insert the SD card and connect the power cable to a power source. Turn on Raspberry Pi 3 and it will boot from your SD card. Raspbmc will now install to your Pi 3.

Don't touch anything while the installation is taking place – it will take about 1 to 25 minutes so leave it to finish, at which point it will boot up to XBMC.

Step 3 – Tweak Your Settings

Nearly there, we just need to change a few settings so that it all runs right. These are the recommended settings:

- **Resolution -** open **Settings>System>Video Output.** Change to the resolution you want – 720p is best.
- **Overscan** – open **Settings>System>Video Output>Video Calibration.** Use the calibration wizard to get the picture fitting the screen
- **System Performance Profile** – open **Programs>Raspbmc Settings>System Configuration.** This is a setting that is specific to the Pi 3, allowing you to overclock so things are a little bit faster. Set it to "Fast" as this will make things speedier but won't affect the stability. "Super" setting runs things even faster but is liable to cause some instability
- **MPEG2 Codec License** – This must be bought via the Raspberry Pi store. Once purchased, open **Programs>Raspbmc Settings>System Configuration** to set it up. You can play videos in MPEG 2 – these cannot be played on the Pi as it is. If you are not using these videos, you can ignore this step.

Your XBMC center is now set and ready to go.

Browser Controlled Robot (Video)

These instructions will allow you to make a simple robot, controlled via video over a browser. You will be able to control your robot using your tablet or smartphone, even via video on your PC. It is also possible to use a gamepad controller for controlling the robot. You can either connect the robot to your own WLAN or connect the controlling device to the robot's WLAN so that you use the robot outside of your home.

What You Will Need

Hardware:

- 4tronix Initio 4WD Robot Kit for Raspberry Pi
- Raspberry Pi 3 Model B
- 2.8mm wide angle lens 1080p HD USB Camera Module
- Raspberry Pi Wi-Fi dongle
- AA NiMH 2300mAh rechargeable battery
- AA battery charger (big enough to charge 6 batteries at the same time)
- DC & Stepper Motor HAT for Raspberry Pi
- 16-Channel PWM / Servo HAT for Raspberry Pi
- 3.3V, 2.6A Step-Down Voltage Regulator D24V22F3
- Logitech Gamepad F710 - optional
- Microsoft Xbox 360 Wireless Controller for Xbox 360 Console - optional
- Microsoft Xbox 360 Wireless Receiver for Windows - optional
- Brass black-plated M2.5 Standoffs for Pi HATs
- GPIO Stacking Header for the Pi A+/B+/Pi 2/Pi 3 with extra-long 2x20 Pins
- Micro USB cable with 20 AWG power lines
- M2,5 / 16mm screw
- M2,5 screw nut
- M2 / 12mm screw
- M2 screw nut
- Shrink tubes or hot glue gun
- 20 AWG Jumper Wires
- Solder

Software and Online Services:

- Microsoft Windows 10 IoT Core
- Microsoft Visual Studio 2015

Software Prerequisites

You will need to use a Windows 10 Client that has a build of a minimum of 14393, along with Visual Studio 2015, Update 3, that has the universal Window App Development tools in it. If you are using the Model B Pi 3, you should use the image for Raspberry Pi Windows IoT Core Build 14393 or above.

Steps to Build:

1. Assemble the robot case but don't connect any of the sensors at this stage. Also, make sure to use the HATs
2. Solder the DC and Stepper motor HAT
3. Solder the GPIO Stacking Header
4. Solder the 16-channel PWM/'Servo HAT
5. Now place the DC and Stepper Motor Hat on the Pi 3 and then put the 16-channel PWM on top of that
6. Now solder the step-down regulator and mount it to your robot. The camera can now be added on the mounting bracket
7. Plug the camera in
8. Add the Wi-Fi dongle and one of the gamepad controllers
9. Wire it all together and solder a custom power cable. Make sure you use the 20 AWG jumper wires for all your power connections
10. Optional – configure the robot-hosted Wi-Fi hotspot

If you want, you can disable the default hotspot from within Windows Device Portal and make your own with PowerShell and the Wi-Fi dongle. Here's how to do that:

1. Open the Windows Device Portal
2. Go to the section titles IoT Onboarding and disable SoftAP

3. Make sure that your dongle is connected to the USB port on the Pi 3

Now you need to change the default name of minwinpc to the name of your own Raspberry Pi in these scripts:

1. Open PowerShell and connect with your Pi device

```
net start WinRM

Set-Item   WSMan:\localhost\Client\TrustedHosts   -
Value minwinpc

Enter-PsSession -ComputerName minwinpc -Credential
minwinpc\Administrator
```

2. Disable the Raspberry Pi onboard WLAN

```
devcon disable *VID_02D0*
```

3. Set up a hosted network and change the name of the WLAN if you need to – ssid= "WLAN name"

4. Change the WLAN key – key=password

```
netsh     wlan     set     hostednetwork     mode=allow
ssid=minwinpc key=p@ssw0rd keyusage=persistent

netsh wlan start hostednetwork
```

5. Create a file called "StartWifiHost.cmd" and then add in this:

```
netsh wlan start hosted network
```

6. Copy this file over to your Pi 3 using Windows Explorer:

```
\\minwinpc\C$
```

7. Go back to PowerShell and create a n new user, giving them admin permissions – make sure to change the password of the user:

```
net user /add WiFiHostServiceUser p@ssw0rd

net localgroup Administrators WiFiHostServiceUser
/add
```

8. Add a new task to Windows Scheduler that will run "StartWifiHost.comd" after booting, ensuring that your WLAN will start on bootup. Make sure you replace password with the user's password:

```
schtasks /create /tn "Start WiFi Host" /tr
C:\StartWifiHost.cmd /sc onstart /ru
WiFiHostServiceUser /rp p@ssw0rd /RL HIGHEST
```

Your hotspot will now start up when your Raspberry Pi 3 reboots and you can connect to WLAN. You will be able to access your Pi 3 using IP address 192.168.1371.

How to Use

After your robot is assembled and the app deployed, with the hosted network properly configured, you may connect to the robot-hosted WLAN. In your mobile device or PC browser, go to http://192.168.137.1. If your robot is connected to your home WLAN, you will need to open http://minwinpc instead (or substitute the name of your Pi 3 if you changed it)

A VPN Server

There is no need to purchase any special equipment to do this; turning your Raspberry Pi 3 into a VPN server is simple. You will need to use LogMeInHamachi to create your VPN so here is what you will need:

- An account at LogMeIn – this is free. Hamachi will create a VPN for you once you have an account so you don't have to waste time with port forwarding, attempting to get past firewalls or with static IP addresses.
- Privoxy – this is an app that pairs with Hamachi to enable secure web browsing, whether it is network-external or network-internal. Instructions to download will be given later.
- Raspberry Pi 3
- An HDMI or composite video cable
- A minimum 8GB Class 10 microSD card, preferably 16 GB
- A card reader – either built-in to your computer or external
- A USB mouse and keyboard
- An Ethernet cable
- A Micro USB power supply

Step 1 – Connecting and Configuring Raspberry Pi 3

By now, your pi 3 should already be installed with Raspbian – if not, go and install it now and change your default keyboard if you are not doing this in the UK Some commands require the use of special characters, and these are in different places on different language keyboards. Once Raspbian is set up, head to the command prompt and type in the following:

```
sudo dpkg-reconfigure keyboard-configuration
```

Follow the prompts on the screen to change your keyboard and then type in the sudo reboot command to restart everything. You can also use this instead:

```
invoke-rc.d keyboard-setup start
```

Step 2 – Update and Install Hamachi

Hamachi will require some extra packages and you might not have them in your image of Raspbian. That means we need to update them so make sure you do not miss this step out – it will save you a whole heap of trouble later. First, type in the following to update:

```
sudo apt-get update
```

Now type in this command so that LSB is installed:

```
sudo apt-get install —fix-missing lsb lsb-core
```

Let it update and then you can go ahead and download Hamachi – type in this command:

```
sudo wget https://secure.logmein.com/labs/logmein-hamachi_2.1.0.86-1_armel.deb
```

To install Hamachi, type this in:

```
sudo dpkg -1 logmein-hamachi_2.1.0.86-1_armel.deb
```

Step 3 – Configure Hamachi

To connect your Pi 3 to your LogMeIn account and to create a new network connection with Hamachi, type in this command on your Pi 3 and run it:

```
sudo hamachi login

sudo hamachi attach [type in your logmein.com email]
```

```
sudo hamachi set-nick [type in a nickname for your
Raspberry Pi 3]
```

On a separate PC, visit LogMeIn and sign in. Go to Networks and click My Networks. You Raspberry Pi 3 is trying to connect and make a brand-new network. Allow it to and write down the 9-digit network ID.

On your Raspberry Pi 3, type in this command:

```
sudo hamachi do-join [type in the network ID you
made a note of]
```

Input your password for LogMeIn and, if needed, go back to the computer and approve the request to join. Your Raspberry Pi 3 is now a part of the Hamachi VPN so go to LogMeIn on the computer and make a note of the virtual IP address that your Pi 3 has been assigned.

Start the SSH server, and to allow remote control of your Raspberry Pi 3, type this command in:

```
sudo /etc/init.d/ssh start
```

Step 4 – Install Hamachi on your PC

We are nearly there now so go to www.vpn.net for Hamachi and download the correct client for your specific computer operating system. Now click Network and then click on Join. SSH into your Pi 3 and access your network files. You will need to use Terminal in Linux or Mac or PuTTY in Windows to SSH into your Pi 3 address.

Step 5 – Optional Step – Install Privoxy

If you want to use your Pi 3 as a proxy server, you must connect Hamachi to Privoxy. This lets you secure and encrypt web browsing when your sessions are over a public Wi-Fi network. This is how you set Privoxy up on your Pi 3:

- Run this command to install Privoxy:
```
sudo apt-get install privoxy
```

- Start Privoxy using this command:
```
etc/init.d/privoxy start
```

- Type in this command to open the configuration file in your text editor:
```
sudo nano /etc/privoxy/config
```

- Look for this line of code:
```
listen-address localhost:8118
```

- Comment the line out by adding a # at the start of it
- Add this line in below that line:
```
listen-address [the IP address that was assigned
to your Pi by Hamachi]:8118 (e.g., 25.1.1.1:8118)
```

- Press CTRL+X - this will save the file and then you can input the following command to restart Privoxy:
```
sudo service privoxy restart
```

Now you just need to set Privoxy as your proxy server on your computer. Here's how you do that:

- **Google Chrome** – Click on Settings>Show Advanced Settings>Network>Change Proxy Settings
- **Firefox** – Click on Preferences>Advanced>Network>Configure How Firefox Connects to the Internet>Settings

Input the IP address that was assigned to Raspberry Pi 3 by Hamachi to the proxy address section and then input the port to 8118

Josh Thompsons

An Airplay Receiver

To turn your Raspberry Pi 3 into an Airplay receiver is very easy but you are going to need a few extra things. Here's your list:

- Raspberry Pi 3
- HDMI cable, or composite
- A minimum 8 GB micro SD card, class 10 or better
- A card reader – external or built-in to your computer
- A USB mouse and keyboard
- A micro USB power supply, minimum 700mA at 5V
- A 3.5 mm stereo audio cable
- A Wi-Fi USB adapter – for you to send music to your Pi 3 from your iOS device
- A USB Sound Card – to give you better sound as the sound that comes out pf Pi 3 isn't brilliant
- A stereo that has speakers that will let you add audio input
- iPhone, iPad or iPod Touch or a computer with iTunes installed as a source of music. If you have an Android device, install DoubleTwist and try it

The Raspberry Pi 3 is one of the best devices suited to being turned into an Airplay receiver and, when you complete this project, you will have a neat device that will connect to your stereo, providing you with functions that are like speakers with Airplay. When you connect up and then boot up, everything that is needed to start Airplay will load automatically so there is no need to attach a monitor or a keyboard. Neat, or what? You won't need to purchase an Airport express because you will be streaming music to any speaker you choose for a small fraction of the cost and, even better, you can continue using your Raspberry Pi 3 for any other project. The only thing you don't get with this is the ability to send Video as there is no support for Airplay Mirroring.

70

Here's how to turn your Raspberry Pi 3 into an Airplay receiver:

Step 1 – Connecting and Configuring Your Raspberry Pi 3

You should already have Raspbian installed on your Pi 3 – this is best one to use the Airplay function with. If you want your Airplay receiver to start without using a keyboard or a monitor, you will need to set Raspbian up so it logs you in automatically. We do this through raspi-config so type this in at the command prompt and find the setting called "Start Desktop on Boot" – you can set this to "Yes". If the rest of your Raspbian is set up, go back to the command prompt and type in this command:

```
sudo raspi-config
```

Next, we need to add some packages that are not likely to be in your specific Raspbian package so type in and execute each of these commands:

```
sudo apt-get update
```

```
sudo apt-get upgrade
```

It will take some time for the update to complete so exercise a little patience and leave it until everything is done. Your Pi 3 will reboot itself and go back to Raspbian; check that everything works like it should and then we can begin to set the Airplay function up. There are two ways to do this; with console commands or, the way we are going to do it, through the Raspbian interface – this is the easier option.

Step 2 Setting Up

- **USB Wi-Fi Adapter**

The first thing to set up is your Wi-Fi adaptor and that is very easy to do through Raspbian:

- Plug your Wi-Fi adapter into your Pi 3 if you haven't already done this
- Go to your desktop computer and open up the configuration application for the Wi-Fi
- There will be a list of options in a drop-down menu; pick your adapter from the list
- Lastly, sign into the network

For the Wi-Fi adaptor, that is all there is to set up. You can, if you want, go to the Midori website on your desktop and check the internet is working. Raspbian is clever in that it will remember what you choose so, even if your adaptor becomes disconnected, when you reconnect it, it will automatically load with the right settings.

- **Your Sound Card**

Next, we need to configure the sound so connect your sound card to your Pi 3 through the USB. Now connect the 3.5mm audio cable to the Pi 3 and then to your stereo. We now need to input a terminal command so go and open the LXTerminal from your desktop and type in the following command:

```
aplay -l
```

You will see something that looks a bit like this on the screen – it will be displayed by your sound card:

```
Card 1: set [device name], devices 0: USB Audio
```

This is telling you that your Raspberry Pi 3 has recognized the card and we can now test the sound from it. To do this, type the following command in:

```
Alsamixer
```

The software the is needed to test the sound will load so, press on the F6 key and choose your specific sound card to change the output type. To test that output, type this command in:

```
speaker-test
```

If there are no problems, you should have sound coming out of your speakers – this will confirm that the sound card is working properly

Finally, we need to make some changes so that the card is automatically loaded when Raspbian boots up. These changes are being made to the configuration file so type the following command in:

```
cd /etc/modprobe.d

sudo nano alsa-base.conf
```

We have specified that we want a file called alsa-base.conf to open, which it now will. Navigate through the file until you get to this line:

```
options snd-usb-audio index=-2
```

At the start of the line, type in a # - this will comment the line out. To save the changes, press CTRL+X and then exit the file

Now, when your Raspberry Pi 3 boots up, both your sound card and the Wi-Fi adaptor will now automatically work:

Step 3 - Install the Shairport Airplay Emulator

Lastly, we must install the software that will make Airplay work. This is going to take a bit of time to set up – it isn't difficult but you do need to allow a good 30 minutes to complete it as there are quite a few bits of software to install. First, before we can even think about Shairport, there are some other things that we need to install so, at the command prompt, type in this:

```
sudo apt-get install git libao-dev libssl-dev
libcrypt-openssl-rsa-perl       libio-socket-inet6-perl
libwww-perl avahi-utils libmodule-build-perl
```

Be patient; this will take a while so leave it be. When it has completed, you will need to install an update so type this command in:

```
git clone https://github.com/njh/perl-net-sdp.git
perl-net-sdp

cd perl-net-sdp

perl Build.PL

sudo ./Build

sudo ./Build test

sudo ./Build install

cd ..
```

When the installation has completed, and this will also take a little while, we can think about installing Shairport. Go back to the Home directory from the command prompt and then type this command in:

```
git                                        clone
https://github.com/hendrikw82/shairport.git

cd shairport

make
```

To run Shairport, type in this command:

```
./shairport.pl -a AirPi
```

In this example, your Raspberry Pi 3 has been named AirPi – you can change the name to whatever you want. On your iPhone, iPod Touch and iPad Air, pick the music app you want to use and tap on the Airplay button. Your Pi 3 will be listed as an output device so tap it and you will hear the music from your sound card.

We haven't quite finished though; Shairport is not going to start automatically when your Pi 3 is booted up so, because we are not adding any peripherals to make it work, we must do just one more thing. At the command prompt, type the following in:

```
cd shairport

make install

cp shairport.init.sample /etc/init.d/shairport

cd /etc/init.d

chmod a+x shairport

update-rc.d shairport defaults
```

Finally, we need to Shairport as a launch item so type this in:

```
sudo nano shairport
```

The Shairport file will load and we need to make a few small changes to it. Look for the line that has DAEMON_ARGS in it and edit it so it reads:

```
DAEMON_ARGS="-w $PIDFILE -a AirPi"
```

Press on CTRL+X to save your changes and exit the file. We are all set up and Shairport will now launch automatically when your Raspberry Pi 3 is booted up, allowing you to take it wherever you want, a truly mobile Airplay device. So long as the Wi-Fi adapter and the sound card are connected, they will both load with Shairport and there is no need for a keyboard, monitor or mouse to be added.

To use Airplay, all you do is connect your Pi 3 to any power source and turn it on. It will take up to about 40 seconds for Raspbian to load and then you can begin streaming your music via your Raspberry Pi 3.

There are other, more complicated projects for to try when you are ready and the following links take you to some of those projects; there are many more to be found on the internet:

1. **A "Magic" Mirror** – Transform an ordinary mirror so it shows you the current time, the weather in your location and the latest headline news
http://michaelteeuw.nl/post/84026273526/and-there-it-is-the-end-result-of-the-magic

2. **A PiPhone** – Make a smart but ordinary mobile phone
http://www.davidhunt.ie/piphone-a-raspberry-pi-based-smartphone/

3. **Games Arcade** – Turn your Raspberry Pi 3 into an all-singing, all-dancing games arcade
https://retropie.org.uk/

4. Install the popular Alexa onto your Raspberry Pi 3 and have your very own voice assistant
https://www.hackster.io/shiva-siddharth/install-alexa-on-raspberry-pi-with-wake-word-and-airplay-15fad4?ref=part&ref_id=19713&offset=3

5. **A Smart Robot** – Build your Raspberry Pi 3 into a robot that has differential GPS www.hackster.io/ingmar-

stapel/raspberry-pi-powered-roboter-with-differential-gps-4ee269?ref=part&ref_id=19713&offset=7

Here are other helpful links to lots more Raspberry Pi 3 Projects:

Raspberry Pi 3 Model B projects: www.hackster.io/raspberry-pi/products/raspberry-pi-3-model-b

10 Surprisingly Practical Raspberry Pi Projects Anybody Can Do: www.pcworld.com/article/3043022/computers/10-surprisingly-practical-raspberry-pi-projects-anybody-can-do.html

Top 10 Raspberry Pi Projects for Beginners: www.lifehacker.com/top-10-raspberry-pi-projects-for-beginners-1791002723

838 Projects Tagged with "Raspberry Pi": www.hackaday.io/projects/tag/raspberry%20pi

10 Projects To Get You Going with the Pi 3: www.techrepublic.com/pictures/the-top-10-projects-to-try-out-with-your-raspberry-pi-3/

25 Fun Things To Do With a Raspberry Pi: www.cnet.com/how-to/25-fun-things-to-do-with-a-raspberry-pi/

Chapter 8: Raspberry Pi 3 Hints and Tips

If you have experience with Linux, these will make sense to you but, if not, these tips are going to help you make the best use of your Pi 3:

- **Command line Completion**

You don't need to type long unwieldy paths, filenames, and commands. All you need to do is type in a couple of characters. Press the Tab key and, if there is an immediate match, Shell will auto-fill it. If there are several options, you should press Tab again and choose the right one from the list

- **Command History**

Bash maintains a history of every command that you type in. From the command prompt, press on the UP arrow and all the commands that you typed in recently will appear. Keep pressing the key until you highlight the one you want; press on Enter to execute that command.

- **Going to the Start or End of a Command**

If you need to get the end or to the start of a command, press CTRL+A to go to the beginning and CTRL+E to get to the end.

- **Alt+F1 to F6 Keys will Switch Screens**

You can easily multitask so long as you are not in the GUI environment. Press on ALT and then the F1 through F6 keys and switch between each of your open terminal windows.

- **sudo !!**

Sometimes you need to be a superuser to execute some commands but you won't always know that so, to save yourself the irritation of trying and failing, type in sudo!! And the last command will get executed as root. If you type in scrot-h, you will see a number of configuration options for scrot and you can change it to how you want it.

- **Screenshots**

Install Scrot by typing in sudo apt-get install scrot at your command prompt and this will allow you to take screenshots while in the graphical user interface, once you have installed scrot, you can execute in your terminal window, saving a .png of the desktop into your working directory.

- **Log in Remotely**

If you want access to your Raspberry Pi 3 command line from a different computer, type in sudo raspi-config. Then select the option that allows you to enable SSH. Once enabled, you can type in ifconfig and you will get access to your Pi 3 IP address. If you use Linux or Mac, type in ssh pi@[ip address] or you can use PuTTY if you are on Windows

- **Single Line Python Web Server**

You can easily create a web server with a single command by typing at the Python command prompt python -m SimpleHTTPServer. Then you can execute it. Every file that is in your working directory will then be accessible through your Pi 3 IP Address

- **raspberrypi.local**

If you find it hard to remember the IP address of your Raspberry Pi 3, especially when you need access to it through your network, simply install avahi. Type in sudo apt-get install avahi-daemon and then execute it. You will now be able to you raspberrypi.local rather than your IP address.

Conclusion

Thank you again for purchasing this book!

I hope this book was able to help you to understand how to get the most out of your Raspberry Pi 3.

The next step is to expand your knowledge and build on what you have learned in this book. There are many more projects for you to discover and build and your learning has just.begun.

Finally, if you enjoyed this book, then I'd like to ask you for a favor, would you be kind enough to leave a review for this book on Amazon? It'd be greatly appreciated!

Thank you and good luck!

Made in the USA
San Bernardino, CA
22 October 2017